Rosa Bonheur

With a Checklist of Works in American Collections

Rosalia Shriver

Philadelphia
The Art Alliance Press
London and Toronto: Associated University Presses

© 1982 by Associated University Presses, Inc.

Associated University Presses, Inc.
4 Cornwall Drive
East Brunswick, N.J. 08816

Associated University Presses Ltd
27 Chancery Lane
London WC2A 1NS, England

Associated University Presses
Toronto M5E 1A7, Canada

Library of Congress Cataloging in Publication Data

Shriver, Rosalia, 1927–
    Rosa Bonheur: with a checklist of works in American
collections.

    Bibliography: p.
    Includes index.
    1. Bonheur, Rosa, 1822–1899.   2. Painters—France—
Biography.   3. Painting, French—United States—Catalogs.
I. Title.
ND553.B6S5   759.4 [B]   81-15047
ISBN 0-87982-037-3   AACR2

Printed in the United States of America

CONTENTS

LIST OF ILLUSTRATIONS

Color Illustrations:

Black-and-White Illustrations:

ACKNOWLEDGMENTS

I would like to thank Mr. Richard H. Hart, former head of the humanities department of the Enoch Pratt Free Library, for his advice and encouragement; Mr. William R. Johnston, assistant director of the Walters Art Gallery, for providing some useful materials; and Miss Joan Quick, who read the typescript and made some helpful suggestions. I am grateful as well to the following museums for their permission to reproduce the illustrations: the Art Institute of Chicago, Chicago, Ill.; the Art Museum, Princeton University, Princeton, N.J.; Brooklyn Museum, Brooklyn, N.Y.; Buffalo Bill Historical Center, Cody, Wyo.; Chrysler Museum at Norfolk, Norfolk, Va.; the Cleveland Museum of Art, Cleveland, Ohio; Columbus Museum of Art, Columbus, Ohio; the Currier Gallery of Art, Manchester, N.H.; the Fine Arts Museums of San Francisco, San Francisco, Calif.; Haussner's Restaurant, Inc., Baltimore, Md.; Herbert F. Johnson Museum of Art, Cornell University, Ithaca, N.Y.; Isabella Stewart Gardner Museum, Boston, Mass.; John and Mable Ringling Museum of Art, Sarasota, Fla.; the Metropolitan Museum of Art, New York, N.Y.; New Orleans Museum of Art, New Orleans, La.; Norton Simon Museum of Art at Pasadena, Pasadena, Calif.; the R. W. Norton Art Gallery, Shreveport, La.; Philadelphia Museum of Art, Philadelphia, Pa.; Phoenix Art Museum, Phoenix, Ariz.; the Reading Public Museum and Art

11

Gallery, Reading, Pa.; San Diego Museum of Art, San Diego, Calif.; Sterling and Francine Clark Art Institute, Williamstown, Mass.; Tweed Museum of Art, University of Minnesota–Duluth, Duluth, Minn.; University of Michigan Museum of Art, Ann Arbor, Mich.; Vassar College Art Gallery, Poughkeepsie, N.Y.; Walters Art Gallery, Baltimore, Md.; the Warner Collection of the Gulf States Paper Corp., Tuscaloosa, Ala.

INTRODUCTION

Rosa Bonheur, one of the nineteenth century's foremost animal painters, has fallen into disfavor as a painter during the last half century, primarily because animal painting itself is no longer highly regarded. Some critics consider her a second-rate artist. In their view, more is wanted than a technically perfect representation of an animal; some "spark of genius" is demanded, some intangible quality that suggests a spiritual connection between man and animal. Yet her work won high praise during her lifetime for that very fidelity to nature. It confirmed the prevalent idea that nature is always true and always beautiful. Her knowledge of animal anatomy, her skillful drawing and modeling, and her ability to portray the special characteristics of a breed were unsurpassed, and these skills reveal how intimately she knew whatever species she was depicting—not only the breed, but the particular animal within that breed.

Rosa Bonheur's life spanned three-quarters of the nineteenth century, a time of conflicting and contradictory views. Art, of course, never exists in a vacuum; it is a concomitant of the social, literary, and philosophical ideas of its era. Thus nineteenth-century art was directly affected by the results of the French Revolution and the Industrial Revolution. The French Revolution had established the idea of the importance of the individual, fostering a trend toward originality, a breaking away from the domination of academic rules. Since it had also swept

13

away the patronage system by suppressing the clergy and dispersing the nobility, the artist was left free to paint as he chose. The Industrial Revolution influenced a return to naturalism. This trend was slower in developing in France than in England, because France itself was slower in becoming industrialized. As the factory owners and merchants of both countries acquired more and more wealth, they were less and less inclined to buy art depicting historical and allegorical subjects that they did not understand.

As if in anticipation of this, in the final years of the eighteenth century the English discovered the Dutch landscape painters, whose subjects everyone understood. Landscape painting became the kind of art people wanted to buy. It was not until the "Salon Anglais" of 1824—so called because thirty English canvases, including John Constable's *Hay Wain,* were exhibited—that the French recognized this. After this salon a new school of art was born in France. The subjectivity of Romanticism replaced the objectivity of Classicism. As these two schools waged their war of ideas, an army of French artists experimented with novel ways of painting.

In 1847 Constant Troyon went to Holland and encountered the animal paintings of such artists as Paul Potter. He returned to France and influenced a whole school of French animal painters. In spite of this Troyon is associated with the Barbizon school of landscapists, with which group Rosa Bonheur never associated herself (those gentlemen lived on the other side of the Forest of Fontainebleau, and apparently Bonheur never met them). As Troyon's popularity grew, so did that of animal painting as an offshoot of realism and landscape painting. The year 1848, the year in which Rosa Bonheur's star was rising, marks the advent of this realistic theme in art. Largely responsible for this was the novelist George Sand, whose writings extolled the virtues and the beauties of the simplicity of peasant life. Bonheur admired George Sand immensely, particularly because of her liberal and socialistic ideas.

The significance of Rosa Bonheur as a nineteenth-century French artist is that she succeeded so admirably in a man's world. Her origins were humble, and she has been described as "a diamond in the rough," yet she was accepted and admired by the nobility of Europe. The Empress Eugénie visited her, as did the prince and princess of Wales. The crown prince of Prussia sought her out, and princes and princesses of Poland were her friends. On the other hand, Bonheur was often criticized for her masculine behavior. Her letters are said to be salty, as was her conversation, and published extracts give a good hint of this. Her life-style with her chosen companions elicited further censure, but she insisted that what she did in her own house was nobody's business but her own.

This remarkable woman was mainly self-educated. Although she was taught by her father, who had some artistic training, Rosa Bonheur never attended formal art classes, and her academic education was sketchy.

At thirty-eight years of age she secluded herself in a country estate, and for the next forty years she worked unremittingly studying, painting, and above all selling her work to an eager world. Bonheur's contribution to nineteenth-century French art is a vast number of paintings, drawings, and watercolors of animals. She labored at her craft with an unswerving dedication throughout almost every one of her seventy-seven years of life. In an interview forty years before her death she expressed a devotion that never changed during all the years that followed:

Art is an absorbent,—a tyrant. It demands heart, brain, soul, body, the entireness of its votary. Nothing less will win its highest favor. I wed art. It is my husband—my world—my life-dream—the air I breathe. I know nothing else—feel nothing else—think nothing else. My soul finds in it the most complete satisfaction. I married art. . . .What could I do with any other husband?[1]

Rosa Bonheur

Bonheur is a French word that has delightful connotations of happiness, prosperity, good fortune, and good luck. It seems providential that it was the surname of Marie Rosalie Bonheur, for she enjoyed all these good things during a long, productive life that began on 16 March 1822 in Bordeaux.

Her ancestors had been cooks, but her father, Oscar Raymond Bonheur, broke this tradition by showing artistic talent at an early age with his imitative drawings of his father's butter and sugar ornaments. He was therefore sent to the Bordeaux Drawing School, where one of his teachers was Pierre Lacour. Eventually Raymond became a teacher himself. One of his pupils was a young lady named Sophie Marquis, whom he married against her parents' wishes.

The origins of Mlle Marquis are a mystery. Although Rosa tried during most of her life to discover her mother's background, she never succeeded. She felt that her mother's mother had been of noble origin and that this fact was known in some way to the nobility. She attributed her warm acceptance by the nobility to this fact. Whatever these origins were, they did not contribute to the Bonheurs' financial success at this time. Together Raymond and Sophie earned only a modest income, he by teaching drawing and she by giving music lessons (she was an adept pianist). Since they lived with his parents, life in Bordeaux was not unpleasant.

Rosa, their first child, began to show her independent characteristics very early. Lively and boisterous, she had a temper as

well. Raymond adored her and thought she showed talent. With
the brushes and pencils he gave her she drew circles and scrib-
bles all over the white walls. He gave her paper and scissors; she
littered the floor with cutouts. Recalling this in later years, she
always liked to say that these cuttings followed the same pat-
tern, in the same order: a shepherd, a dog, a cow, a sheep, a
tree. She was as uninhibited as she was uncorrected, eliciting
from her grandfather the remark that although they thought they
had a daughter, Rosa was really a boy in petticoats.[2]

In 1824 Auguste was born, and in 1827 Isidore. Since Bordeaux did not seem to offer enough opportunities to support a
family of seven, Raymond decided to go·to Paris, where he
hoped there would be more work and more money. In 1828 he
left his family in Bordeaux and went to Paris. It was only at the
end of a year that he sent for his family to join him. Because he
was ill, the grandfather remained behind. He died in 1829.

When the Bonheurs arrived in the capital, most of the new
inhabitants lived around the edges of town, where the lodgings
were cheaper and nearer to the great industrial centers that were
growing up. In those early years of the nineteenth century rich
and poor lived in the same localities, forming a democratic and
tolerant mosaic.[3]

Life was little better in Paris. Rosa hated it: the weather was
cold and wet, the city was big and noisy, and even the bread,
that glory of Western civilization, seemed insipid to her, because
unlike that of Bordeaux it was unsalted. The new house was in
the Rue Saint-Antoine, across the street from a pork butcher,
and on the ground floor of their building was a public bath.

Having no fields in which to play, the children resorted to the
Place Royale, today's Place des Vosges. The other boys tried to
drive Rosa away with the usual cry of "no girls," but Rosa was
used to playing with her brothers and soon enforced with her
fists her right to be there. Soon she became not only their playmate, but their leader as well.

It was there that she first met her lifelong companion, Nathalie
Micas. Poor Nathalie was not only a girl, but a frail and sickly
one at that. She wore silly clothes and a green eyeshade. The
children made her life miserable with the particular cruelty that
small children know so well how to inflict. Life plays strange
tricks; no one could have foreseen that these two different little
girls would later become inseparable friends.

Very near this house in the Rue Saint-Antoine was a school taught by a Father Antin, a Jansenist, whose advanced ideas included educating girls with boys at a time when it was unusual for girls to go to school at all. Rosa was sent to class with her brothers. It had a lasting effect. In her memoirs of many years later she said that the school life imposed a masculine tendency upon her character, although it lasted a mere three years, until 1830.

In that year two momentous events occurred. The first was the Revolution of 1830, in consequence of which Charles X fled and Louis Philippe was proclaimed king. The second event was the birth to the Bonheurs of a second daughter and fourth child, Juliette. It is no exaggeration to say that Juliette was born to the sound of the guns of the July Revolution; there was a cannon at the very door of the house firing on the Place de la Bastille down the street.

This revolution accomplished more for the middle class than had the Revolution of 1789: the separation between church and state was realized, the hereditary house of peers was replaced by a nominated house, and the vote was extended. However, domestic conditions—those affecting the Bonheurs—worsened. In addition to a severe winter, increased unemployment and widespread financial distress made economic conditions difficult. Raymond had fewer students than ever. The family moved to a cheaper apartment in the Rue des Tournelles. This house had a long, dark staircase that frightened the children because there was an undertaker's establishment on the ground floor.

In 1832, when Rosa was ten, they moved yet again, to a house in the Rue du Helder that was farther west, but farther too from Father Antin's school, the Place Royale, and Nathalie. The move had been made necessary by a cholera epidemic.

The cholera had begun its deadly journey westward from the Ganges in August of 1817. It took its first Parisian victim from the Rue Mazarine on 26 March 1832, then struck the Faubourg Saint-Antoine, then the Faubourg Saint-Honoré. Quickly, indiscriminately, it attacked the entire city; during the following month, April 1832, alone, 12,700 persons died. It was an appalling death that usually came after only a few hours of intense suffering. The patient's skin turned a dark blue, his body became icy cold, and he suffered agonies of cramps and convulsions.[4] At night the death carts made their grisly rounds, amassing the bodies of the dead, just as they had done during the Black Death. The remembrance of those awesome wagons haunted Rosa into her old age. If a family moved from one quarter of the city to escape the epidemic, it would soon find them in another. Then as suddenly as the disease had come it left. Miraculously, the Bonheurs had survived. Paris instituted some sanitary reforms, such as paving lanes and opening up the more crowded areas; however, as late as 1848, when Louis Napoleon arrived, Paris was still a city of congested alleys and sordid courtyards, profuse with filth and fetid odors.

A further upheaval—if it can be called that—befell the family in 1833. Influenced by friends and his own idealism, Raymond joined the society of the Saint-Simonians. This group, whose ideas had been formulated by Claude Saint-Simon, advocated a kind of religious socialism. Among their tenets were the abolition of the law of inheritance, the enfranchisement of women, and the complete equality of women with men. Moreover, they believed in a feminine element of the Godhead and anticipated the coming of a female messiah. Their ideal for society was a world based on love, in which class distinctions would be abolished and in which man would be placed according to his ability and awarded accordingly. In such a utopia all war would cease.

Raymond Bonheur, impressionable and idealistic, was neither a philosopher nor an original thinker but an artist of limited education. Yet he allied himself with this group and left his family for a second time to live in the pseudomonastic fellowship at Ménilmontant. There menial domestic tasks were allocated to each man regardless of his social position. The men wore a peculiar costume, said to have been designed by Raymond, which consisted of white trousers, red waistcoat, and violet blue tunic, each of which had a symbolic meaning. For example, the waistcoat fastened in the back with hooks and eyes, so that the men had to help each other to dress. This act, they felt, increased their feeling of communality and dependence on each other.

As a family, the Bonheurs supported Raymond wholeheartedly in this venture. They believed in his ideas with as much fervor as he. The liberal tenets of Saint-Simonianism remained with Rosa Bonheur all of her life, molding her into the independent, forceful character that she was.

On the other hand, it was a difficult time for them. They were without a breadwinner, and Sophie had to struggle to feed the family. Although Ménilmontant was some distance from their home, they all went to visit once a week wearing their Saint-Simonian hats with large tassels. These hats provoked derision from the children in the streets, but this minor persecution only strengthened their devotion.

The sect was not only an annoyance to the government but a political threat as well, and it was a source of unrest among the people. Consequently, the society was tried on a specious charge and the commune at Ménilmontant was forced to disband.

Raymond returned home, but Sophie, worn out with years of constant care and privation, died shortly afterward. She was buried in a pauper's grave. For all of Rosa's life it was a source of sorrow to her that she never knew the location of her mother's grave.

Since the grandmother had died in 1831 and Raymond was forced to be away from home most of the day, he was obliged to find someone to care for the children. The first attempt was to put them in the care of a nurse named Mère Catherine in the Champs Elysées. Afterwards, he sent little Juliette to live with a friend in Bordeaux. He put the boys in a boarding school where their tuition was paid for by his art lessons in the same school. Then, knowing how hard the life of an artist is, he decided that his elder daughter should be trained as a dressmaker. He reckoned without Rosa.

Mme Gendorf the dressmaker had a husband who made percussion caps for hunting rifles. While the other girls worked on their stitches, Rosa sneaked away to help Monsieur. She liked to turn the crank on one of the lathes. Mme Gendorf sent her recalcitrant apprentice back to Papa.

As a conscientious father, Raymond wanted Rosa to grow up with an adequate education, so the next attempt was to send her to Mme Gilbert's boarding school in the Rue de Reuilly. Rosa was a charity pupil—or, more euphemistically, a scholarship pupil—since her father also taught drawing at this school in return for her tuition.

As was the custom then, the girls brought their own eating utensils, and while the others had silver knives and forks and drinking cups, Rosa's were of a far simpler material. While they had pretty, expensive dresses and plenty of pocket money, Rosa did not. One can be sure that her companions did not let Rosa forget her lowly status. Such conditions are unbearable for a little girl. Like any miserable child with a strong personality, Rosa reacted violently. Her disposition was "turbulent, even fierce," and her temper became ungovernable. She led the girls into wild games that resulted in the destruction of the flower beds and Mme Gilbert's pride and joy, the rose garden. Again, she was sent home. This time Raymond bowed to fate and allowed her to remain.

While Raymond was away during the day Rosa occupied herself by copying the casts in the studio and doing other drawing. She worked consistently by herself, happy to be doing what she really wanted to do, that which she was destined to do. One day on his return her father found her completing her first real painting, a study of a bunch of cherries, and was so delighted that he undertook her artistic training. So, at the age of thirteen, her formal education—such as it had been—ended, and she became a regular art student.

Many dictionaries and encyclopedias quote the Salon catalog of an early date to the effect that she was a pupil of Léon Cogniet. She always denied this, saying that she was the pupil of her father only. The reason for the discrepancy is that, when the catalog with this statement first appeared, M. Cogniet wrote her a note saying that he would have been delighted to have had her as a pupil. She was so touched by his courtesy that she could not bring herself to contradict the Salon.

The next phase of her training was standard procedure for the time. She went to the Louvre and copied the paintings of the masters. The nonstandard aspect of this was that she was a girl. Although her presence invited laughter not only from the other students, but from some of the visitors as well, she was not deterred but often spent the whole day at the museum. Occasionally, she was able to sell one of her paintings. This small sum was added to the money she was making by doing some work for M. and Mme Bisson, who did heraldic paintings. Neither activity brought in very much, but the few sous that she did earn were a cause of some pride and eked out the meager wages of her father.

About 1836 a man called on Raymond and asked him to paint a portrait of his daughter. To Rosa's surprise and embarrassment, the daughter was her former playmate, Nathalie. Disregarding past differences, the girls developed a friendship that was to last for the rest of their lives. The obvious affection between the two caused the Micases to take such an intense interest in Rosa that they ended by adopting her.

The Micases were a well-to-do family. M. Micas had a leather business, and Mme Micas had a shop in which twenty people were employed making eyeglass cases. The reason they had approached Raymond for a portrait was that Nathalie was still in very delicate health and they fully expected her death in the near future.

The 1840s were a momentous decade for the family, for they marked Rosa's first exhibitions at the Salon. Rosa had discovered that she enjoyed painting animals more than anything else. In 1841 it was decided that she was ready to exhibit her first paintings, so she submitted a study of rabbits eating carrots and a drawing of goats and sheep. Later in the same year the family moved to the Rue Rumford, where they had a large studio on the sixth floor above their apartment. Near the fields and farms the neighborhood afforded ample opportunities for the study of farm animals. By now the family had traversed Paris completely from east to west, from the ancient Bastille quarter to the open fields of Villiers and the still-wild Bois de Boulogne. Here they could study animals in their natural surroundings, and Rosa could indulge her taste for the countryside.

Besides the animals outdoors, the Bonheurs kept a small barnyard in the studio itself, housing rabbits, quail, ducks, several kinds of birds, a goat, a squirrel, and even a sheep. The sheep lived on the leads, but Isidore would carry it up and down the six flights of stairs on his shoulders so that it could get some exercise outside.

It was an unusual atmosphere in which to grow up. With very little feminine companionship, but with single-minded dedication, the young woman worked side by side with her father and two brothers honing the skills of her craft. The disorder of the apartment full of animals was not improved by Raymond's casual attitude toward housekeeping and money. Whenever he was paid for something, he would throw the money into the litter on the floor. When a few pennies were needed—to pay for a meal, for example—the children rooted around to find them.

In 1842 this impractical dreamer remarried. The lady was Mme Marguerite Peyrol, a widow from Auvergne, who had a son, Hippolyte. The children's name for her was *Mamiche,* an Auvergne word for "Mother." She wasted no time in putting some order into this very disorderly household and attempted, with small success, to bring a touch of femininity into Rosa's bearing.

For this year's Salon Rosa submitted two pictures of horses and began some paintings on fans and vases, which brought in a little more money.

Anyone who could imagine a place more horrible than a slaughterhouse for an animal lover to frequent would be very imaginative indeed. But that was precisely where Rosa chose to go in 1845. It was an environment in which she could study prize animals in every conceivable state—of repose, of fear, and even of death. Her determination and perseverance to learn in the face of these conditions overcame her natural repugnance.

Besides the lowing and bleating of the terrified animals, the stench of the pent-up beasts, the heat, and the pools of blood on the floor, her sensibilities were offended by seeing them killed. In addition, there was another difficulty. Other animal painters had subjected themselves to such a course of study, but no woman ever had. So the cattle drovers and butchers, a coarse lot anyway, might be excused for their ribaldry and jeers, but often their remarks brought Rosa close to tears. One day a protector arrived in the person of Emile Gravel. He was a huge and power-ful man, a scalder of hides and a packer of pig's feet. Noticing her distress, he lent his size to the force of his words by threaten-ing her tormentors with instant bodily harm if they did not leave her alone. After that Rosa drew in peace.

That evening Rosa's father went to thank M. Gravel for his kindness, and a friendship ensued that was beneficial to the pov-erty-stricken Bonheurs. M. Gravel introduced them to some of his acquaintances, such as the butcher, who would pay for Rosa's pictures with meats, and another man who supplied the artists with canvas.

For the Salon of 1845 Rosa had five pictures ready, and this time she was awarded a third-class medal. The pictures were

The Three Musketeers, Sheep and Lambs Lost during a Storm, Ploughing, Ram—Sheep—Lamb, and *Cows at Pasture.* These five brought the number of her pictures that had been exhibited to eighteen, not an insignificant figure for a twenty-three-year-old woman.

The following year marked an important trip to the Auvergne with Mme Bonheur. They visited Cantal, and among the many sketches that Rosa made, those for *Red Oxen of Cantal* were probably the most valuable. When the painting was finally exhibited in 1848, Rosa's reputation was firmly established. The picture itself was bought by an Englishman for six hundred pounds.[5]

Two other important events occurred this year. Juliette came home and joined the throng in the parental studio in the Rue Rumford. Mme Bonheur's son Hippolyte also came to Paris and was apprenticed to the sculptor Antoine-Louis Barye, the master of "les animaliers."

Juliette was twelve years younger than Rosa. A portrait of her painted by Rosa when Juliette was sixteen shows a charming young lady dressed in silk with her hair arranged in a chignon. She looks completely feminine—quite different from her famous sister.

Although she attended the same school in the Rue de Reuilly from which Rosa was expelled, Juliette succumbed to the family obsession and studied painting with her father. She achieved a degree of success as well. In 1853 a still life was accepted by the Salon, and in 1858 another of her pictures received honorable mention. Her highest honor was a third-class medal awarded in 1889.

Juliette married her stepbrother Hippolyte Peyrol in 1852, and from 1849 until 1860 she taught in the Girls' Drawing School, of which Rosa was directress. Her first son, Hippolyte, was born in 1856 and René in 1860. Both of them became artists. She died in 1891, seven years before Rosa.

In February of 1848 the working classes of Paris revolted once more. They claimed that Louis Philippe had prevented the reestablishment of the 1830 Republic. After only one day of struggle the royal army abandoned the capital, and Louis Philippe, the last of the French kings, abdicated and fled to London.

One important outcome of the revolution concerned the Salon. Instead of a governmental jury, the artists formed their own jury and that year decided that nothing submitted would be rejected. Some of the men on the committee were Horace Vernet, Robert-Fleury, Léon Cogniet, and Jean Baptiste Camille Corot. Their action gave an opportunity to some geniuses to be seen after years of rejections by the official jury; but since 5,180 paintings were accepted, it meant that any daub was hung. The mélange was ludicrous, and it was the last time such a thing was attempted.

Rosa submitted two small bronzes of a bull and a sheep and six paintings, including *Red Oxen of Cantal*. This was the last important work done at the Rue Rumford studio. In appreciation of it the government presented her with an exquisite Sèvres vase and commissioned another work. She chose to do *Plowing in the Nivernais*.

Partly as a result of his daughter's achievement, Raymond Bonheur was finally acknowledged by the government and was given the directorship of the Girls' Drawing School. However, like his first wife, he had been exhausted by hard work and anxiety over his large family. On 24 March 1849 he died of the heart disease from which he had been suffering for the last three years.

With the advance payment of fifteen hundred francs from the government Rosa paid for the cost of her father's funeral. Although he had known of the commission and had seen the work in an unfinished state, Raymond could not share in Rosa's pride when it was finally hung in the Luxembourg. On the other hand, he had at least known that this beloved daughter had equaled, if not surpassed, the model that he had always held up to her, that of Mme Vigée-Lebrun. Thinking of this would comfort Rosa in the years to follow whenever she alluded to her father's ambition for her.

Known primarily as a portrait painter and landscapist, Raymond Bonheur had exhibited his works at the Salon twelve times during the 1830s and 1840s. Although never a great artist, he worked conscientiously as a teacher, and one of his greatest students was his daughter.[6]

Plowing in the Nivernais, or *Labourage Nivernais,* now in the Musée National du Château de Fontainebleau, is perhaps the most important Bonheur work in a European collection. In her biography, *Rosa Bonheur, sa vie, son oeuvre,* Miss Klumpke said that she thought there might be a second version, but she did not know where it was. In fact, there are at least two other versions; one is in the Ringling Museum in Sarasota, Florida, and the other at the R. W. Norton Art Gallery in Shreveport, Louisiana. Differences are apparent in size and in the left background.

The picture has elicited as much praise as *The Horse Fair* for its fidelity to nature and realism. Those who have never seen a team of oxen plowing a field may be unable to appreciate it fully, but contemporary accounts abound of people who stood transfixed before the canvas and said, like one rustic, "Those are oxen! And that is plowing!"

In the year of the 1848 Salon Isidore was twenty-one and according to the law was subject to military service. The Bonheurs could not afford to pay someone to serve for him—a common practice then—so in spite of all attempts to contact influential persons through their acquaintances, Isidore did serve. He was Rosa's favorite brother; her nickname for him was *Dodore*. Like his brothers and sisters, Isidore began his studies in his father's studio, but later was admitted to the Ecole des Beaux Arts.

Isidore made his debut in 1846 when he submitted a painting and a sculpture group of the same subject, *An African Horseman Attacked by a Lioness*. Because she was so devoted to him and did not want wish to detract from his success, Rosa officially abandoned sculpture from that date. From this first Salon on he exhibited regularly, but devoted his talent exclusively to sculpture. He won two medals, one in 1865 and another in 1869. In 1889 he was awarded the coveted gold medal at the Exposition Universelle.

Isidore is best known for his small groups of sculpture. A very appealing work is the beautiful little goose drinking from a bucket, measuring only two and one-half inches in height, in the Walters Art Gallery in Baltimore, Maryland. His two largest commissions were a monument to Rosa at Fontainebleau and the two lions that adorn the steps of the Palais de Justice in Paris.

Isidore had to wait much longer than his famous sister to be admitted to the Legion of Honor, receiving this distinction only in 1894, when he was sixty-seven. The biographies do not say very much about this favorite brother. He never married, but apparently spent his life modeling exquisite little animal statues, most of which were edited by the Peyrols. Having established his right to be counted among that special group known as "les animaliers," Isidore died on 19 November 1901.[7]

In 1849 Rosa Bonheur moved to the Rue d'Assas, where she and the Micases had the whole house including the courtyard and the garden. Mrs. Ellet in her book *Women Artists in All Ages and Countries* describes this place in detail, emphasizing the change in Bonheur's fortunes:

> At the southern end of the Rue d'Assas—a retired street, half made up of extensive gardens, the tops of trees alone visible above the high stone walls—just where, meeting the Rue Vaugirard, it widens into an irregular little square, surrounded by sleepy-looking, old-fashioned houses, and looked down upon by the shining gray roofs and belfry of an ancient Carmelite convent—is a green garden-door, surmounted by the number "32." . . . The house, a long, cozy, irregular building, standing at right angles with the street, is covered with vines, honeysuckles, and clematis. A part of the garden is laid out in flower-beds; but the larger portion—fenced off with a green paling, graveled, and containing several sheds—is given up to the animals kept by the artist as her models. There may be seen a horse, a donkey, four or five goats, sheep of different breeds, ducks, cochinchinas, and other denizens of the barn-yard, all living together in perfect amity and good-will.[8]

In June 1850 Rosa and Nathalie went on their first trip together, to the Pyrenees, to take the baths at several spas in the mountains. Nathalie was very ill, and the cure had been ordered by her doctors. Travel in those days was difficult, and the accommodations were deplorable. At one place the beds were too small, and at another there were so many mice running about that the young women bribed the pests with bread in order to keep them away from themselves. The strange scenery and inhabitants provided material for lots of sketches, but the baths helped very little if at all, and after a few weeks they returned to Paris.

After settling down again in the Rue d'Assas, Bonheur started to frequent the horse market in preparation for the great painting that she was contemplating. This environment was no better than the slaughterhouse for an unaccompanied young woman. It was at that time that Bonheur started to wear masculine attire, which not only facilitated her work but also served as a disguise. Her general demeanor, in combination with the peasant costume that she adopted, accorded so well that most of the people who met her thought that she was a man. Although she was only about five feet tall, her height was average for a woman in those days. Her hair was a dark brown, her eyes almost black, and she had a high forehead, a large nose, and a firm chin. She no longer needed a M. Gravel.

Bonheur spent eighteen months of preparatory work on *The Horse Fair*. Besides the market itself, she obtained permission to work at the Paris Omnibus Company, where she studied the workhorses that pulled the buses through the city.

The original canvas for the painting measured 96¼″ by 199⁷⁄₁₆″, and the horses are two-thirds life-size. When it was finally finished and exhibited at the Salon of 1853, its creator was only thirty-one years old. Yet no other woman had ever achieved a work of such force and brilliance; and no other animal painter had produced a work of such size. Bonheur would labor for another forty-six years, but this painting would remain her masterpiece.

The location of the horse market depicted in the painting was the Boulevard de l'Hôpital near the Salpêtrière. The cupola in the distance is that of the asylum's chapel. Rosa Bonheur has been criticized since, as she was criticized then, for her sketchy treatments of backgrounds and landscapes. As a matter of fact, this was a criticism directed at many of the animal painters of the nineteenth century. Many painters, such as Edwin Landseer, took time to remedy this defect and to study landscape as a separate discipline, and Bonheur did the same with *The Horse Fair*. She repainted parts of the trees and sky, which is why the picture has two dates—1853 and 1855.[9]

However *The Horse Fair*'s background might be faulted, few quibbled with her treatment of the horses. These great beasts are painted with verve and spirit, and the almost-photographic realism reveals her deep understanding of animal anatomy. These are no Thoroughbreds, but workhorses—solid, heavy, and hirsute. The atmosphere is nearly palpable. As the powerful horses rear and plunge and their handlers strain to control them in what seems to be a near-stampede, one can almost hear the shouting and snorting and feel the ground shake under the assault of the hooves. Yet the whole scene is suffused with a lovely, clear sunlight.

After this exhibit, the Salon declared her *hors de concours* or exempt from having to submit future entries to the jury.

In 1853 *The Horse Fair* was sent to the Society of Artists of Ghent, where it had great success but was not sold. Instead, Ghent gave her a cameo representing the painting. Bonheur wanted Bordeaux to have it, since that was her native city, and she offered it to them for twelve thousand francs. The city fathers thought the sum too high for a painting done by a woman, and they refused the artist's offer.

Rosa was not at home when Ernest Gambart, a Belgian art dealer who was established in London, came to the house and offered to buy *The Horse Fair* and take it to England. Nathalie was there, and she flatly refused to let it go for less than forty thousand francs, especially if it were to leave the country. Without a murmur Gambart accepted the price, even though he knew that Bordeaux had already refused to pay twelve thousand francs for the painting. When Rosa found out what had happened, she was overwhelmed by the price her work had brought.

Gambart's plan was to send the painting to Thomas Landseer, the engraver and brother of Sir Edwin Landseer, so that he could make an engraving. With her characteristic generosity, Rosa offered to make a smaller copy that would fit more easily into the engraver's studio and to let Gambart have both pictures for his forty thousand francs. This copy was duly finished, but it was one quarter the size of the original and was largely the work of Nathalie. Rosa had added only the finishing touches.

Then Gambart suggested a trip to England. He, Rosa, and Nathalie would accompany the original painting on an extensive tour of England and Scotland while the smaller version was at Landseer's studio. Rosa was apprehensive; she did not speak English, and she had the habitual reluctance of the French to leave their country. But Gambart was persuasive. He offered a set of inducements that he knew would appeal to her. First he tantalized her with visions of Walter Scott's homeland, which she had loved in imagination since girlhood, and in addition he promised that she would be able to meet Sir Edwin Landseer, whom she admired so much. Swayed, she acquiesced.

In July 1856 she and Nathalie accompanied Gambart across the Channel. Their trip was a *succès fou*. When they arrived in London under the wing of Gambart—who Rosa said was the best traveling companion imaginable—they were greeted with enthusiasm. Londoners flocked to the gallery to see this famous picture painted by a woman. Even Queen Victoria had asked to see *The Horse Fair,* so it had been transported to the palace and brought back to the French Gallery in Pall Mall. This fact alone assured success, and it enhanced Gambart's reputation immeasurably, so that he rose to the height of his fame after the summer of 1856. London, fashionable London, was anxious to meet Rosa Bonheur. The rumor that she wore pants had gone before her. But she had more sense and taste than that. In public she wore a rather severe skirt and jacket of black velvet embroidered in gold.

One of the highlights of the trip was a grand dinner given by Sir Charles and Lady Eastlake, who were the "royalty" of the London art world; he had been keeper of the National Gallery and was president of the Royal Academy. It was at this dinner that Rosa Bonheur finally met her idol. Their interest in each other was observed and Bonheur was genuinely attracted, but she was still the same woman who was later quoted as saying that the only males she liked were the bulls that she painted.[10]

Edwin Landseer was the son of John Landseer, an engraver, who was his son's first and severest teacher. From the time that Edwin, as a small boy, attempted to draw animals in the field, his father insisted that he get it right. The hard lessons were learned, and Edwin became England's most popular painter of animals in more than a century. He eclipsed for a time that other great painter of horses, George Stubbs. Today, however, Stubbs is considered the greater artist. He never sentimentalized or humanized animals as Landseer did. The mawkishness of so much of Sir Edwin's work—such as *The Old Shepherd's Chief Mourner*—is what has caused his decline in the twentieth century. Even *The Monarch of the Glen* is too romanticized. Yet the Victorians doted on them all. Landseer was lionized and he loved it. By nature a bon vivant, he cultivated the highborn and powerful. If he had spent more time at his easel and less in other people's country houses, he might have achieved true greatness. In any case, in 1856 he was at his pinnacle, and Bonheur admired his work tremendously.[11]

Cannily, Gambart had planned a "royal progress." From London they traveled north by easy stages, visiting other English cities. They were always lavishly entertained. The French women were astounded by the numerous, bountiful meals that the English ate, and they entered into all experiences whole-heartedly, even a visit to an iron foundry. When at last they arrived in Scotland, their enthusiasm was unbounded. It was not only the scenery that enchanted them, but the people of every class as well. Like all tourists they wanted to see and to do everything, and, like an indulgent parent, Gambart obliged.

One of the few annoyances was the unexpected attention. Rosa Bonheur was as disturbed by the admiring crowds that followed them everywhere as some movie stars and members of royalty are today. She complained of being watched at Falkirk. But here she was distracted by other interests. The strange Highland animals fascinated her so much that she bought a bull, two cows, and a calf. All this livestock was shipped to Gambart's English house, but unfortunately the animals could not be exported to France because of customs regulations. However, Bonheur made dozens of sketches that resulted in many later paintings, such as *The Stampede, After a Storm in the Highlands,* and *Scottish Shepherd.* The orders for pictures were overwhelming. From this date onward Nathalie's judgment proved correct; their financial future was secure.[12]

After five weeks of traveling they returned from Great Britain in September with portfolios crammed with studies.

The small menagerie at the Rue d'Assas has already been mentioned, but there was also an otter who had a habit of getting out of his tank at night and climbing into Nathalie's bed. Of all bedfellows, a soaking-wet otter seems the least appealing, yet Nathalie never complained, for she was as fond of the animals as was Rosa. Indeed, in order to live with Rosa, one had to love them. Over the years there were many other species. If Rosa did not own them, she borrowed them; it was a widespread practice among animal painters and sculptors of the nineteenth century to exchange models among themselves as they needed them.[13]

Besides her painting, Rosa was working during these years as directress of the Girls' Drawing School, having succeeded her father. This mode of life in Paris continued until 12 June 1860, when the household in the Rue d'Assas moved to By in the Forest of Fontainebleau.

The purchase of this estate was a joint venture of Rosa

Bonheur and the Micases. This was not just because of their mutual preference, but partly in obedience to the will of Nathalie's father. When he died in 1847, he asked them to promise to stay together, even requesting that the first to die should leave her estate to the survivor.

By is the name of the château as well as the hamlet. The next largest town was Thomery, which was then a half hour's drive away. The estate consisted of three hectares, or about seven and one-half acres, which gave them plenty of room for a farm and for stables and pens for the animals, to say nothing of privacy, which was the real reason for the move. Unlike Landseer, Bonheur did not like society. Had she been a portrait painter, seclusion would have been impossible, but in the country she could paint her animals without interference.

The house itself was somewhat small to be ennobled with the term *château*. In fact, it had only two stories. An ancient building dating back from 1400, it had belonged to a royal beekeeper with the droll name of Bigre, which means "hang it" or "confound it." As is the way with names, this one evolved from *Bigre* to *Bige* to *By*.[14] Because of the small size of the house, Bonheur had an atelier built to her own specifications. Later, at the time of her death, she was supervising the construction of a second and larger studio and the installation of electricity so that she could work at night. However, she died before this was completed. In 1860 she made other modifications such as changing the chapel into an orangery; formal religious practice was not a Bonheur strong point.

So began a strange ménage à trois. Mme Micas, who had maintained her own business while her husband lived, performed the function of manager in this household just as efficiently. She was a very good cook and proud of it. She was thrifty, too; she made mattresses from the wool of the forty sheep that Rosa kept at By. Although her education was limited—it is said that she never had a really firm grip on the exigencies of the French language—she knew how to make her "daughters" comfortable. Rosa was deeply devoted to her.

Jeanne-Sarah-Nathalie had a better education than Rosa. Her letters show a true literary flair, and she was a competent artist as well. At least two of her pictures were accepted by the Salon; one in 1853 was a still life, and one in 1865 was entitled *Une*

Basse Cour. In England she was appreciated for her paintings of birds. She dabbled in science, even mechanics; one of her most famous inventions was a railroad brake. In spite of many successful attempts to demonstrate its virtues, and many letters to influential people, she could never sell it. The principal reason, apparently, was that no one could believe that a woman could possibly have invented a functioning mechanical device such as a railroad brake. Financially this endeavor was a failure as far as Nathalie was concerned. It is interesting to note, however, that later a man added an insignificant adjustment to her plan, sold it, and made money.

Other interests of Nathalie's involved medicine and surgery. She enjoyed doctoring the animals and did a good job at that, too.

Without Nathalie, Rosa could never have devoted her life to her art to the extent that she did. She acted as a buffer by keeping people away, a practice that helped alienate members of the Bonheur family. The worst aspect of their relationship was Nathalie's ungovernable jealousy. Family and friends had to contrive ways to avoid offending her, but Rosa's love for her was so great that she put up with it.

At By, Rosa's daily costume consisted of a type of peasant trousers of a dark red shade and a large blue smock braided in white and tight at the wrists. Oblivious to most feminine finery like jewels and laces, she was very vain of her unusually small hands and feet, and liked to wear pretty shoes. At Nathalie's suggestion, she cut her hair short, which, although not the fashion, was becoming. It was a practical costume in view of the life she led in the forest, in fields, and in the studio. Apparently she never wore suits tailored in the latest fashion, as George Sand did. It was scandalous enough for a woman of her era to wear pants at all, but Rosa always did what she preferred, and she preferred pants—just as she preferred to smoke cigarettes and to ride her horse astride. These were some of her ways of asserting that women had a right to their own lives and that they should not be subject to the dictates of society or custom or the dominance of a husband.

The Tedescos—a father and three sons—became Rosa's Paris agents, and they were very successful in selling her canvases. The commissions came in so fast that an ordinary person would have felt pressured. However, no amount of money could induce Bonheur to hurry or to part with a canvas until she was completely satisfied with it. Often she kept patrons waiting two years as the underpainting dried. She used many palettes—some perfectly clean, some covered with numerous coatings of mixed colors, which allowed her to judge certain effects over a period of time. Equally careful of her brushes, she liked to wash them herself, rinsing them again and again until she was satisfied that all trace of soap was gone.

Ernest Gambart was her second agent, in London, as well as the editor of her engravings. He also had the right to all proceeds from engravings of *The Horse Fair* as part of the forty-thousand-franc transaction.

The story of *The Horse Fair* is a complicated one, and accounts of it differ. The original had been sold by Gambart to William P. Wright, and by him to A. T. Stewart, the department-store executive. It was then put up at auction and bought for $55,000 by Cornelius Vanderbilt, who gave it to the Metropolitan Museum in New York. The smaller picture that Thomas Landseer had used was bought by Jacob Bell, who willed it to the National Gallery in London. This fact caused conflicting emotions in the artist. She was pleased that the great English gallery had one of her works, but she was disappointed that it was only a copy; therefore she painted a second version and offered it to the National Gallery. However, they could not accept it because of the terms of Mr. Bell's will. This second version, or third painting, was eventually sold at auction. In all, then, there are three oil paintings, one drawing (not counting the many studies), and a watercolor. The engravings made from Thomas Landseer's plate and others are too numerous to count.

On the afternoon of 14 June 1864 Rosa and her brother-in-law Hippolyte were in the studio smoking an after-luncheon cigarette when they heard a great clatter in the driveway. Rosa was furious because she had explicitly told the servants that she did not wish to be disturbed. One flustered maid stammered that the Empress Eugénie and many ladies and gentlemen had arrived. Rosa was wearing her studio costume; suddenly it was her turn to be flustered. As she struggled to cover her smock and trousers with a dress, the top button caught, and there was just time to make her presentable before the empress swept into the studio with her ladies of honor, officers, and gentlemen. Rosa had been working on her *Les Cerfs sur les longs rochers*. (This particular painting figured at the Exposition of 1867 under the English title *Deer Crossing an Open Space* and was engraved by Charles G. Lewis under the title *Family of Deer Crossing the Summit of the Long Rock [Forest of Fontainebleau]*.) The empress admired this and asked to see other pictures. She then commissioned a painting for herself to be entitled *Sheep at the Edge of the Sea*. Like *Les Cerfs sur les longs rochers,* this painting was exhibited at the Exposition of 1867, after which it went to the Tuilleries. In her biography Anna Klumpke says that Rosa did not know what became of it after 4 September 1870 and the Commune. Actually, the Norton Simon Museum in Pasadena, California, has a painting of this subject and this title dated 1865.

That afternoon Rosa Bonheur escorted the empress to her carriage, and because Eugénie had been so gracious and kind Rosa impulsively kissed her hand. Far from being offended at what might have been considered a forward gesture, Eugénie embraced Rosa in turn. It was an extraordinary mark of approval on the part of the Spanish princess.

Another example of Rosa's character in regard to nobility is that she never allowed herself to be intimated by their superior position—even someone like the princess de Metternich, who tried on several occasions to disconcert Rosa. For example, Rosa refused to answer the princess's letters. One day the princess paid a surprise visit to the studio and asked for a picture, any picture, in return for some bottles of excellent wine from the Metternichs' celebrated cellars. Rosa haughtily replied that the disposition of her paintings could only be arranged through her agents. The princess went away empty-handed.

The most historic day in Rosa Bonheur's life occurred on 10 June 1865, a year after Eugénie's first visit, when she paid a second visit to By. This time they had been informed that the empress was coming, for the occasion was too important to risk missing the celebrated artist.

Louis Napoleon, who had refused to award the Legion of Honor to Rosa Bonheur because she was a woman, had nevertheless been persuaded to allow Eugénie in her role as regent to present it to Rosa in the emperor's absence. Juliette was with her sister that day. In due course, the empress and her court arrived. The story is told that the decoration lacked a pin, so a search was made for this humble object. One of the officers discovered one on a work table, and the ribbon was attached to Rosa's blouse. Thus, Rosa Bonheur became the first woman of France to receive this illustrious award.

The Franco-Prussian War began in 1870 when France refused to allow Prussia to put a Hohenzollern on the throne of Spain. Bismarck wanted a war anyway, so that he could consolidate the German states, and did his best to precipitate matters. As has happened so often, Germany was far better prepared than France, but it was France who attacked Germany on 19 July 1870.

On 4 September the forces of Napoleon were defeated, and the Germans advanced as far as the gates of Paris. The city was blockaded and almost all communication with the outside world stopped.

When he had redesigned the city, Baron Haussmann had tried to forestall future insurrections within the city by broadening the boulevards. In doing so, he demolished old houses and neighbor-hoods without a thought for history or sentiment, and changed the character of the whole city. He had built a thirty-foot wall that encircled Paris for forty miles around. At strategic places along the walls were barracks, which would have been very effective for firing down those grand boulevards against a rioting populace, but which were less effective for protecting the city against an advancing army. Beyond the wall was a ten-foot moat. With fortifications like these, it was no difficult task for the Germans to cut off Paris from the rest of France from September 1870 until April 1871.

At By, Rosa fretted and fumed. She made plans to blow up parts of the château, to kill the animals and eat them—after she had painted them. She declared that she would burn the fodder and pour out the wine to prevent the Germans from using them. She went out dressed in her trousers, shotgun in hand, and pre-pared to muster the men of the village into a militia to defend the ford in the river against the advancing enemy.

She was only dissuaded from this course of action when the mayor of By pointed out to her that the Germans might burn the village in retaliation. He persuaded her to go home, to care for

the wounded soldiers, and to feed the villagers. She did go
home, and she did put away her gun, but she cried like a child in
frustration. Then she rallied her spirits and fed the people soup.
As conditions continued to worsen, Gambart sent her huge bags
of grain for the animals.

In Paris itself, food was so scarce that the inhabitants began to
eat the horses. As the autumn advanced, Edmond de Goncourt
chronicled the day-to-day deterioration in his journal. This effete
gentleman, who had turned up a fastidious nose at horsemeat
during the early days, succumbed to hunger by the end of October. On 29 October he noted that he had donkey steak for dinner. The poorer Parisians were eating rats, but Goncourt on 31
December had elephant-blood sausage for dinner.[15] Indeed,
many people, if they could afford it, were eating the exotic meat
provided by the zoo. Bread was so drastically rationed that if
one were invited to dinner, one took one's morsel along.

Many artists had fled the country. Pissarro, for instance, had
gone to London, leaving fifteen hundred pictures at his house in
Louveciennes. They were all destroyed, for the enemy used his
house as a butchery.[16] Auguste Bonheur's house was completely
ruined.

However, so highly was Rosa Bonheur's art regarded in Germany that her house was protected by order of the crown prince
of Prussia. After hostilities ended, Frederick went to By and
asked permission to come in and see the studio. Rosa refused.
The prince argued that he had protected her and therefore
should be permitted to enter. Independent as always, Rosa re-
torted that he was still the enemy of her country. Frederick went
away without seeing the inside of the house that he had protected.

The decade of the 1870s, which had opened so inauspiciously,
continued in a fairly tranquil way for the residents of By. Miraculously, France was able to pay off the heavy war indemnity
demanded of her by Germany; the National Assembly, the government established after the war, was replaced by the Third
Republic in 1875, and for the next sixty-five years, or until 1940,
the country had at last a stable regime.

With the help of Gambart, who was now the Spanish consul at
Nice, Rosa and Nathalie bought a house there where they spent
the months from December to May. One of Rosa's chief amuse-

ments at Nice was to go to the zoo, where she sketched the wild animals, particularly the lions.

In 1880 Gambart sent two lions from Marseille to By. Nero and his mate consumed twenty pounds of meat a day. After about two months at By they developed a disease, which forced Rosa to give them to the Jardin des Plantes in Paris. Shortly thereafter they both died. Later, she acquired a second lioness named Fathma, and a real affection developed between the two. Fathma was almost like a dog. But after a time this lioness also became ill. Rosa wrote that one day, when she was on the second floor of the house, she heard a noise on the stairs. It was the lioness trying to get to her. Rosa went down to meet her and, sitting on the steps, held the great beast in her arms while she died. Rosa was hearbroken. She insisted that the lioness had really loved her, and that people who say that animals have no souls are less noble than the beasts, because Fathma had shown that she really loved, and nothing can love without a soul.

Rosa Bonheur's religious convictions had been formed in large part by her father's association with the Saint-Simonians, but on the whole she was not a religious person. While not a pantheist, since she did believe in God, she might be described as an agnostic who thought that the migration of souls was probable. In her biography Anna Klumpke quoted some prayers that are parodies of the great prayers of the Church, which were among Rosa's papers. They express the artist's convictions and reflect the influence of Saint-Simonianism. In the parody of the Ave the earth is addressed rather than the Virgin Mary; in the Pater the Father is begged to allow his love to transform the earth; and in the Credo Christ is referred to as "couple," a reflection of the belief that there was a feminine component of the Godhead.[17]

The decade of the 1880s held great sorrow for Rosa Bonheur. In 1882 her young half-brother Germain died of the effects of his war service in 1870. This young man, the son of Marguerite and Raymond, had been born in 1849. Like all Bonheurs he was an artist and had been a pupil of Gerôme. He exhibited landscapes at the Salon from 1874 until 1879. His wife was the sister of another artist, Ulysée Besnard. They had no children.

Then on 22 February 1884 Auguste, her eldest brother, died. Auguste worked very hard all his life. His pictures were mellower, rather prettier than Rosa's, but like hers were almost always of animals in landscapes. Although he attained the rank of chevalier of the Legion of Honor in 1867, he was over-shadowed by his famous sister. He had married in 1851 and left five children.

The greatest grief of all was the death of Nathalie on 22 June 1889. It was as if part of her own soul had left her. After many weeks she forced herself to work again, but it was not until Anna Klumpke came to paint her portrait that her life would take on meaning again.

Anna Elizabeth Klumpke entered Rosa Bonheur's life for the first time in 1887. She had been born in San Francisco, California, in 1856, the oldest of four unusually gifted sisters. When they were very young their mother took the girls to Europe, where they were educated. Anna was a talented artist. Admitted to the Academie Julien, she studied under Tony Robert-Fleury, and on visits to the Luxembourg Gallery had an opportunity to study and to copy Rosa Bonheur's great *Plowing in the Niver-nais*.

Sometime during the summer of 1887, Anna attended a party where she met John Arbuckle, another admirer of Bonheur's work. Far off in Wyoming he had heard that the artist wanted to study the wild ponies of the western plains, and had sent one to her. Since many months had elapsed and he had not heard from her, he wondered if the horse had ever arrived. Since he was in France on other business, he wanted to call at By and inquire. The only stumbling block was that he could not speak French. Anna offered to go with him and act as interpreter. The two went to Fontainebleau, but Rosa and Nathalie were at Nice. The servant who received them assured them that a horse had indeed arrived, but that it was so wild they could do nothing with it. She offered to show it to them. In the stables, Mr. Arbuckle and Miss Klumpke saw his horse, but they were a little alarmed by the presence of a lion in the barnyard. The servant seemed to take a perverse glee in proving how gentle the lion was in comparison to the wild pony. Having satisfied themselves about the mus-tang, and being more than a little apprehensive about the lion, the two Americans backed away and returned to Paris.

In 1889, the year of the Universal Exposition, Buffalo Bill brought his Wild West Show to Paris. Col. William Frederick

Cody, who had had a long and colorful career before this date, had been born in the Kansas Territory in 1846. He had been successively a Pony Express rider, a soldier with the Union army, an Indian fighter, a provider of buffalo meat to the railroad builders—whence his nickname—and finally a showman. The trip to Paris was his second European venture. His first trip to England in 1887, the year of Queen Victoria's jubilee year, had been a spectacular success.

Almost all of the crowned heads of Europe had attended the show in London, and Queen Victoria herself was so curious to see it that she made an unprecedented trip from Windsor. Thousands of Englishmen crammed the vast arena daily. Drawn partly by curiosity to see an authentic bit of American life, and largely by the approbation of the royal family, the people were enthralled. They saw exhibitions of horsemanship by cowboys and Indians; they saw dazzling feats of markmanship by Annie Oakley; and they saw re-creations of American history such as Indian attacks on a stagecoach and wagon train, as well as a reenactment of Custer's Last Stand.[18] The enchanted Europeans lined Bill Cody's pockets with gold.

Just as reports of this extravaganza had drawn the reclusive Victoria from Windsor, so did it draw the hermit Rosa Bonheur from By. Not only did it offer a chance to observe some strange men such as *les peaux-rouges,* the redskins, but it included such exotic animals as bison and mustangs.

During the seven months that the show was in Paris, Rosa spent most of her time at the site of the camp. This provided a diversion for her after the weeks of intense grief caused by the death of Nathalie. Productive as always, she painted about seventeen pictures of Indians, buffalo, and cowboys.

However, the most famous painting that she produced was not done at the camp, but at By. On 25 September 1889 Cody went there for a visit, and Rosa painted a majestic picture of him mounted on his horse. The painting was widely reproduced in posters and all sorts of promotional literature and eventually sent home to his wife. The original is now at the Buffalo Bill Historical Center in Cody, Wyoming.

John Arbuckle was in Paris again in 1889, and this time he and Anna Klumpke were invited to luncheon at By. Rosa was very apologetic. She explained that she had received two other ponies from another admirer at the same time and had assumed that all three had come from the same person. Belatedly, Mr. Arbuckle was thanked. Bonheur had good reason to be apologetic: just the day before, Bill Cody's men had removed the troublesome mustang, whose name was Apache, as well as another pony with the endearing name of Clair de Lune.

After this luncheon Anna Klumpke's life took another tack; although nothing changed immediately, nothing was ever the same again.

Klumpke had already made a name for herself in the world of art. In 1887 she had painted a portrait of Elizabeth Cady Stanton, the noted feminist and mother of Theodore Stanton, the author of *Reminiscences of Rosa Bonheur*. This portrait had been exhibited at the Salon of 1887 together with a portrait of Anna Klumpke's mother. Between 1889 and 1898 Klumpke established her own studio in Boston and strengthened her reputation by teaching and exhibiting in America as well as in France.

In 1897 she wrote to Rosa Bonheur requesting permission to paint a portrait of the older artist. It was almost a year before she received a letter granting this permission. Arriving in the spring of the year, Klumpke expected to travel between Paris and By, as Bonheur wanted to grant only a few hours a day to the sittings. As the painting progressed, Anna wanted to consult her former teacher, Robert-Fleury, on the progress of her work. Rosa was slightly miffed, and convinced Anna that she was just as well qualified a judge. She offered to teach Anna herself, and by July she had grown so fond of the younger woman that she begged her to remain at By permanently.[19] At first Anna demurred, citing obligations to her own family and wondering what other people would say. Rosa replied emphatically that she did not care what other people thought—she had always done what she wanted to do—and repeated that she had come to love Anna deeply. The family obligations could be taken care of. Anna stayed and became the pupil and companion of the artist whom she admired profoundly. In later years she referred to Rosa as "the illustrious woman whose precious maternal tenderness will remain forever the most glorious event of my life."[20]

During the remaining months of Rosa's life, Anna finished two portraits of her. The first, which shows Rosa holding some drawings and a brush, is the property of the Metropolitan Museum in

New York. The second shows Rosa holding her little white dog, Charley, and was exhibited in 1899.

On 9 November 1898 Rosa rewrote her will appointing Anna chief executrix and leaving to her the major part of her property with the exception of a few minor bequests to members of her family and the servants. Then on 28 November 1898 she wrote a letter explaining why she had done this and emphasizing that Anna had not coerced her in any way. She explained that she had helped her family financially all of her life, not only by gifts of money but by paying for the education of their children. Anna, she continued, had given up her own career in order to stay with her out of sincere affection, and her motives were in no way mercenary.

Some members of the family remained unconvinced, and a lawsuit contesting the will followed Rosa's death. However, the will was found to be valid.

At Christmastime of that year of 1898 Anna arranged a Christmas pageant at the primary school in By. This was a small school that Rosa and Nathalie had established so that the children of the village would be spared a long ride to and from Thomery twice a day. When the idea was first proposed, the parents were dubious about the little boys and girls attending classes together, but the fact that they were relieved of the fatigue of commuting changed their minds.

Christmas pageants as Anna knew them were not familiar to Rosa, but Rosa was anxious to have one when Anna explained how they were done in America. Consequently, Rosa Bonheur's last Christmas on earth had an American flavor.

Rosa and Anna went to the school, where a large Christmas tree was the primary decoration. There were gifts for the children from the adults, and songs for the adults from the children. As foundress, Rosa was the guest of honor, and Miss Klumpke says in her book that Rosa enjoyed this touch of America in the midst of the Forest of Fontainebleau.

During the winter of 1899 Bonheur was involved in two great projects, both of which remained unfinished at the time of her death. One was a painting entitled *Wheat Threshing*. It was a large painting and was giving her trouble. She asked Henri Cain, a longtime friend and fellow artist, to help with the sky. Anna Klumpke also assisted with it. Probably because of its size, the picture was never finished. The other project was the construction of the new and larger studio with its installation of electricity.

Anna Klumpke relates that on the day Rosa became ill she had been outside conferring with the workmen. Since it was a raw day and Bonheur was lightly dressed, she caught a chill. By afternoon she was feeling so unwell that she went to bed. The final illness lasted only a few days, and on 25 May 1899 Rosa Bonheur died.

At the church in Thomery she was given a Catholic funeral. Then her body was transferred to Père Lachaise Cemetery in Paris, and she was buried beside her beloved Nathalie in the Micases' vault. There were no speeches and no military honors, although she would have been entitled to them as an officer of the Legion of Honor.[21] This was the way she wished it. On her tomb is the inscription: *L'Amitié est une affection divine.*[22]

AFTERWORD

When Anna Klumpke undertook to dispose of the studio's contents she expected the sale to bring in about three hundred thousand francs, basing her opinion on the few works with which she was familiar. The Tedesco brothers assured her that the total number of drawings would bring in more than a million. They said that they and their father had been trying to get hold of these drawings for years, but that Mlle Bonheur would never sell them because she wanted to keep them for reference so that she could check her progress from time to time.

As they dismantled the studio, Klumpke was dumbfounded. Not only were there 892 paintings, but box after box of drawings was unearthed, with everything sorted and dated according to category. The total number of these drawings varies from source to source, but the final number is about two thousand.

The sale was held at the Galerie George Petit in the Rue de Sèze during the last week of May and the first week of June 1900, and lasted nine days. The 892 paintings brought 956,121 francs, and the drawings grossed 1,180,880 francs.[23]

Even Anna Klumpke, writing as early as 1908, said that it would impossible to tell where all the works were. They had been dispersed in the course of a lifetime and, as a result of the sale, to the four corners of the world. They are owned by galleries and museums and private collectors. The Checklist indicates some of the public galleries which own works of Rosa Bonheur and whose directors and curators were kind enough to respond to my request for information.

NOTES

1. "A Morning with Rosa Bonheur," *The Living Age* 802, 3d series no. 79 (8 October 1859): 124–26.
2. Theodore Stanton, *Reminiscences of Rosa Bonheur*, p. 16.
3. Marcel Raval, *Histoire de Paris*, p. 98.
4. Louis Blanc, *History of Ten Years* 1: 613–14.
5. "Rosa Bonheur," *Chambers's Journal* 19, no. 483 (4 April 1863): 219.
6. Emile Bellier de la Chavignerie, *Dictionnaire General*, p. 115.
7. Ibid., p. 116.
8. Elizabeth Fries Ellet, *Women Artists in All Ages and Countries*, pp. 277–78.
9. New York [City] Metropolitan Museum of Art, *A Catalog of French Paintings*, 2: 161.
10. Stanton, p. 366.
11. Campbell Lennie, *Landseer: The Victorian Paragon*, p. 8.
12. *Lippincott's Magazine* 75 (1905): 464.
13. *Apollo* 104 (October 1976): 301.
14. Anna E. Klumpke, *Rosa Bonheur, sa vie, son oeuvre*, p. 244.
15. George Becker, *Paris under Siege, 1870–1871*, pp. 127, 186.
16. James Laver, *French Painting and the Nineteenth Century*, p. 85.
17. Klumpke, p. 85.
18. Don Russell, *The Lives and Legends of Buffalo Bill*, p. 332.
19. Klumpke, p. 150.
20. Clara Erskine Clement, *Women in the Fine Arts from the Seventh Century B.C. to the Twentieth Century A.D.*, p. 198.
21. In 1894 Rosa Bonheur sent four pictures to America to the Chicago Exposition: *King of the Forest, Bouscalade, Pastorale* (bought by Jay Gould), and *Sheep*. For these paintings she was awarded the rank of officer of the Legion of Honor. This, her highest honor, completed a very long list of awards and honors.
22. "Friendship is a divine affection."
23. "The Rosa Bonheur Sale," *The Art Journal* 52 (1900): 222–23.

BIBLIOGRAPHY

Books

Becker, George J., trans. and ed. *Paris under Siege, 1870–1871. From the Goncourt Journal*. With a historical introduction by Paul H. Beik. Ithaca, N.Y.: Cornell University Press, 1969.

Bellier de la Chavignerie, Emile. *Dictionnaire Général des Artistes de l'Ecole Française depuis l'origine des arts du dessin jusqu'à nos jours*. Paris: Librarie Renouard, 1882.

Benezit, E. *Dictionnaire des Peintres, Sculpteurs, Dessinateurs et Graveurs*. Nouvelle edition. Paris: Librarie Grund, 1976.

Blanc, Louis. *The History of Ten Years, 1830–1840*. 2 vols. Reprints of Economic Classics. New York: Augustus M. Kelley, 1969.

Clement, Clara Erskine. *Women in the Fine Arts from the Seventh Century B.C. to the Twentieth Century A.D.* Boston: Houghton, Mifflin, 1904. Reprint. New York: Hacker Art Books, 1974.

Ellet, Mrs. Elizabeth Fries. *Women Artists in All Ages and Countries*. New York: Harper & Bros., 1859.

Hamerton, Philip Gilbert. *Contemporary French Painters: An Essay*. London: Seeley, Jackson and Halliday, 1868.

Klumpke, Anna E. *Rosa Bonheur, sa vie, son oeuvre*. Paris: Flammarion, 1908.

Lepelle de Bois-Gallais, F. *Memoir of Mademoiselle Rosa Bonheur*. Translated by James Parry. New York: Williams, Stevens, Williams, 1857.

Laver, James. *French Painting and the Nineteenth Century.* London: B. T. Batsford, 1937.

Lennie, Campbell. *Landseer: The Victorian Paragon.* London: Hamish Hamilton, 1976.

New York [City] Metropolitan Museum of Art. *A Catalog of French Paintings.* Vol. 2: *XIX Century,* by Charles Sterling and Margaretta M. Salinger. New York: The Metropolitan Museum of Art, 1966.

Raval, Marcel. *Histoire de Paris.* "Que Sais-Je?" Paris: Presses Universitaires de France, 1948.

Roger-Miles, Leon Octave-Jean. *Atelier Rosa Bonheur.* Paris: Georges Petit, 1900.

Russell, Don. *The Lives and Legends of Buffalo Bill.* Norman: University of Oklahoma Press, 1960.

Stanton, Theodore. *Reminiscences of Rosa Bonheur.* New York: Appleton, 1910. Reprint. New York: Hacker Art Books, 1976.

Stranahan, Clara Cornelia. *A History of French Painting from Its Earliest to Its Latest Practice.* New York: Scribner's, 1888.

Articles

Bacon, Henry. "Rosa Bonheur." *Century Magazine* 28 (1884): 833–40.

Bentzon, Th. [Mme. Blanc]. Translated from the French by Bellina Phillips. "Rosa Bonheur." *Outlook* 62 (6 May 1899): 41–49.

Bonheur, Rosa. "The Story of My Life." *Ladies' Home Journal,* December 1896, pp. 13–14.

Bonheur, Rosa. "Fragments of My Autobiography." *Magazine of Art* 26 (1902): 531–36.

Bull, H. A. "Notes of the Month: Bonheur Museum—Fontainebleau." *International Studio* 94 (December 1929): 73–74.

Chu, Petra ten-Doesschate. "Unsuspected Pleasures in Artists' Letters" [in the Lugt Collection]. *Apollo,* n.s. 104 (October 1976): 298–305.

Claretie, Jules. "Rosa Bonheur: An Appreciation with Some Hitherto Unpublished Studies." *Harper's Magazine* 104 (December 1901): 136–46.

Forbes-Robertson, John. "Rosa Bonheur." *Magazine of Art* 5 (1882): 45–50.

Holme, George. "Rosa Bonheur." *Munsey's Magazine* 11 (April 1894): 58–65.

Mehard, René. "Rosa Bonheur." *The Portfolio* 6 (1875): 98–101.

Stanton, Theodore. "The Greatest of Women Painters: Rosa Bonheur's First Visit to England and Scotland." *Lippincott's Monthly Magazine* 75 (1905): 461–64.

"The Dominant Masculinity of Rosa Bonheur." *Current Literature* 50 (4 February 1911): 207–10. [A review of T. Stanton's book.]

"Mlle. Rosa Bonheur." *Athenaeum,* no. 3736, 3 June 1899, p. 695. [An obituary.]

"A Morning with Rosa Bonheur." *The Living Age* 802, 3d series no. 79 (8 October 1859): 124–26.

"Rosa Bonheur." *Chambers's Journal* 19, no. 483 (4 April 1863): 218–20.

"Rosa Bonheur Sale." *The Art Journal* 52 (1900): 222–23.

"Rosa Bonheur's Most Famous Painting, *The Horse Fair.*" *Ladies' Home Journal* 27 (1 November 1910): 10–11.

"How America Made Rosa Bonheur." *Ladies' Home Journal* 28 (1 March 1911): 11.

"Rosa Bonheur's Centenary." *International Studio* 75 (1922): 367–72.

"Rosa Bonheur." *Leisure Hour* 10 (1861): 359–62.

CHECKLIST

In American Collections:

Alabama

Tuscaloosa. Warner Collection of Gulf States Paper Corp.
King of the Forest: oil on canvas 97″ × 68½″, Geraldine Rockefeller Dodge.
The Duel: oil on canvas 59″ × 96″, acquired from Sotheby Parke Bernet 1976, sale 3872 lot 18.

Arizona

Phoenix. Phoenix Art Museum.
Untitled (horse): oil on canvas 8¾″ × 11″, collection of Phoenix Art Museum, bequest of the estate of Dr. Patricia Lynch.

California

Pasadena. Norton Simon Museum of Art at Pasadena.
Sheep by the Sea: oil on cradled panel 1865, signed lower left: R. Bonheur 12½″ × 18″.
San Diego. San Diego Museum of Art.
Horse's Legs: pencil drawing 13″ × 8½″.
Bovine Head: pencil drawing 12″ × 16⅛″.
Reclining Bovine: pencil drawing 8¹¹⁄₁₆″ × 13½″.

51

San Francisco. Fine Arts Museums of San Francisco.

Male Figure Studies: ca. 1850–57. A Donkey Driver (Un Bourriquaire), soft graphite with stumping, heightened with white chalk on moderately thick blue wove handmade paper. Slightly foxed and faded. Stamp in rose ink on verso: 1903. 18¾" × 12⁵⁄₁₆" (47.6cm × 31.3cm). Atelier stamp, lower right: Rosa B. (Lugt 2147)

Study of Two Male Figures: soft graphite with stumping heightened with white chalk on moderately thick blue wove handmade paper. Stamp in rose ink on verso: 1903. 12¼" × 18⁵⁄₈" (31.2cm × 47.3cm). Atelier stamp, lower right: Rosa B. (Lugt 2147). Gift of René A. May.

Head of a Royal Tiger: ca. 1878. Graphite on thick cream wove paper 9⁷⁄₁₆" × 7¹³⁄₁₆". (23.9cm × 19.9cm). Atelier stamp in black ink, lower right: Rosa Bonheur (Lugt 275).

Lioness's Heads: ca. 1865–84. Graphite under black chalk on thick cream laid paper flecked with brown and gray fibers, with right deckled edge and watermark: Michallet 9" × 11⁵⁄₈" (22.8cm × 29.6cm). Atelier stamp in black ink, lower right: Rosa Bonheur (Lugt 275).

Stag on the Watch (Cerf aux aguets): ca. 1883. Graphite under watercolor on thick cream wove paper with two deckled edges. 9⁹⁄₁₆" × 11⅞" (23.0cm × 30.1cm). Numerical notations on verso: in orange chalk, R/924: in graphite, no. 1007. Atelier stamp in black ink, lower right: Rosa Bonheur (Lugt 274).

Santa Barbara. The museum mentions a pastel 1897, *Migration of the Bison* 44" × 74½", in a private collection.

Stockton. Pioneer Museum and Haggin Galleries.

Bergerie: unsigned lithograph 5³⁄₁₆" × 9¹¹⁄₁₆" (comp.).

Untitled: 1880, oil on canvas 25⅞" × 21½", Haggin Collection (landscape, two fawns in forest, one standing and one lying down). Signed lower left: Rosa Bonheur 1880.

Harvest Season: oil on canvas 16¾" × 32¼" (sight) Haggin Collection. Signed lower left: Rosa Bonheur.

Gathering for the Hunt: oil on canvas 30½" × 58⅛" (sight) Haggin Collection. Signed lower right: Rosa Bonheur 1856.

Connecticut

Hartford. Wadsworth Atheneum.

Bull: bronze sculpture, 10⅞" length, given by Samuel P. Avery in 1920.

Florida

Sarasota. John and Mable Ringling Museum of Art.
Labourages Nivernais: canvas 52½″ × 102″. Coll. Viscount Hambledon, sold at Christie's London, March 1929, No. 177. Signed: Rosa Bonheur 1850.
A Family of Deer Crossing the Summit of the Long Rocks in the Forest of Fontainebleau: canvas 54½″ × 128″.

Illinois

Chicago. Art Institute of Chicago.
Cattle at Rest on a Hillside in the Alps: oil on canvas 55cm × 66.4cm. A. A. Munger Coll. 1901. Signed: Rosa Bonheur 1885.

Louisiana

New Orleans. New Orleans Museum of Art.
Deer on the Alert: oil on canvas 25″ × 28¼″ framed, 15¼″ × 18¼″ unframed. Signed lower left: Rosa Bonheur 1887.
Shreveport. The R. W. Norton Art Gallery.
Boeufs et taureaux de la race du Cantal, dated 1888 oil on canvas, 25″ × 39″ (*see* Anna Klumpke, *Rosa Bonheur, sa vie, son oeuvre,* p. 193: caption to illus. indicates the painting won a 1st class medal at the Paris salon of 1848, but since the painting in Shreveport is dated 40 years later, either this was a misprint or the painting is a copy by R.B.)
La Fenaison en Auvergne: dated 1855, oil on board, 8⅝″ × 16⅛″ (*see* Klumpke, p. 228).
Le Labourage Nivernais: dated 1849, oil on board, 8½″ × 16⅛″(*see* Klumpke, p. 196 [note] and p. 198).
Muletiers des Pyrénées: dated 1882, oil on canvas 26″ × 32⅛″ (*see* Klumpke, p. 205).
Shepherd and Sheep: dated 1858, sepia wash drawing 12″ × 18″.
Studies of Dogs: pencil 10¼″ × 16¾″.
Sculpture in Bronze (height precedes length)
  Cow: 3¼″ × 5½″
  Bull: 3″ × 5″
  Bull Reclining: 5¼″ × 11½″ (inscribed: Peyrol [Rosa's brother-in-law, who cast this bronze]).

Ewe Grazing: 5½″ × 8¼″ (two examples, one of which has a golden patina).

Maryland

Baltimore. Haussner's Restaurant.
Calves: oil on canvas 10½″ × 13½″.
Baltimore. Walters Art Gallery.
Plowing Scene: oil on canvas, signed at lower left: Rosa Bonheur 1854. 19½″ × 31¾″ (49.5cm × 80.5cm).
Andalusian Bulls: wash heightened with white 15″ × 9″ (sight). Signed at lower right: R. Bonheur 1867.
Sketch of five bulls, with color notes; pencil on tracing paper, color notes in blue and red watercolor; gray mat 9″ × 14⅞″ (sight).
The Conversation: charcoal on paper 14½″ × 21¾″ (sight). Signed at lower right: Rosa Bonheur.

Massachusetts

Boston. Isabella Stewart Gardner Museum.
A She-Goat: oil on canvas 10″ × 12¾″ (0.25cm × 0.32cm). Signed lower left: Rosa Bonheur.
Williamstown. Sterling and Francine Clark Art Institute.
Bull Resting: soft black pencil 11¾″ × 17¼″. Atelier stamp, lower right: Rosa Bonheur.
Studies of a Lioness: graphite on white wove paper glued onto heavy mat board 6⁹⁄₁₆″ × 9²³⁄₃₂″. Gift of Denison B. Hull.
Study of a Lion's Head: graphite on gray wove paper 6²¹⁄₃₂″ × 10²³⁄₃₂″. Gift of Denison B. Hull.

Michigan

Ann Arbor. The University of Michigan Museum of Art.
Head of a Dog: oil 12⅛″ × 16½″. Signed: Rosa Bonheur 1878. Gift of Mr. Jean A. Wetmore, 1919.
Detroit. The Detroit Institute of Arts.
Deer in Repose: canvas 41″ × 33″. Signed lower left: Rosa Bonheur 1867. Gift of Avery Coonley 1920.

Minnesota

Duluth. University of Minnesota, Tweed Museum of Art.
Two Horses: oil on canvas 28½" × 39½".
Steers at the Gate: oil on canvas 21" × 27⅞".

Missouri

Saint Louis. The Saint Louis Art Museum.
Relay Hunting: oil on canvas 18" × 26". Signed lower left:
Rosa Bonheur 1887.

New Hampshire

Manchester. The Currier Gallery of Art.
Does at Rest: oil on canvas 13⅛" × 25⅜" (66cm × 81.5cm).
Signed lower left: Rosa Bonheur. Bequest from George Leighton in 1918. Mr. Leighton purchased it from the New Galleries in 1914, Los Angeles, California.

New Jersey

Princeton. The Art Museum, Princeton University.
White Horse: oil on canvas, 54cm × 65.3cm. Signed lower left. Seal: Vente Rosa Bonheur 1900.
Study of a Dog: oil on canvas, 33.3cm × 28.2cm. Signed lower left. Seal: Vente Rosa Bonheur 1900. Gift of Stuart P. Feld, Class of 1957 and Mrs. Feld, in 1976.
Warrior Driving Chariot: pencil on ivory paper.
Studies of Horsemen: pencil on ivory paper.

New York

Brooklyn. The Brooklyn Museum.
Study of a Bull's Head: small watercolor 5⅛" × 7¹/₁₆".
Buffalo. State University of New York at Buffalo.
Still Life: Asparagus: canvas mounted on board 7¼" × 10¼" (18.4cm × 26cm), unsigned.
Still Life: Green Onions: canvas mounted on board 5⅞" × 10½" (14.8cm × 26.3cm), unsigned.
Still Life: Radishes: canvas mounted on board 7" × 7½" (17.9cm × 19cm), unsigned.
  These three are mounted in one frame, ascribed to Bonheur.

Ithaca. Herbert F. Johnson Museum of Art, Cornell University.
 Young Bulls: Planographic lithograph 8″ × 11¼″. Pencil: Rosa
 Bonheur, n.d. Bequest of William P. Chapman.
New York. The Metropolitan Museum of Art.
 The Horse Fair: oil on canvas 96¼″ × 199½″ (244.5cm ×
 406.8cm). Signed lower right: Rosa Bonheur 1853–5.
 Weaning the Calves: oil on canvas 25⅝″ × 32″ (65.1cm ×
 81.3cm). Signed lower left: Rosa Bonheur 1879.
 A Limier Briquet Hound: oil on canvas 14½″ × 18″ (36.8cm ×
 45.7cm). Signed lower right R. B.
 Landscape with Cattle: black lead pencil on blue paper faded
 to gray 9⅛″ × 12⅛″. Gift of Helen Wormaer, 1963.
 Study for "The Horse Fair": black chalk, gray wash height-
 ened with white on beige paper 5⅜″ × 13¼″. Bequest of Edith
 H. Proskauer, 1975.
Poughkeepsie. Vassar College Art Gallery.
 Stag Listening to the Wind: oil on canvas 31¾″ × 39½″.
 Signed lower left: R. Bonheur 1867. Sale stamp.

Ohio

Cincinnati. Cincinnati Art Museum.
 Cowherd: oil on canvas 60½″ × 45⅜″. Signed lower right. Gift
 of Carl J. Schmid.
Cleveland. The Cleveland Museum of Art.
 Recumbent Stag: watercolor on paper 11″ × 15″ (28cm ×
 38.1cm.)
 Sheep: brown, white and pink wash over pencil on gray paper
 8³⁄₁₆″ × 12⁹⁄₁₆″ (20.9cm × 31.9cm). Signed and dated 1861.
 Farmyard: oil on paper on canvas 11³⁄₁₆″ × 15⅞″ (28.4cm ×
 40.3cm). Signed lower left: Rosa Bonheur.
Columbus. The Columbus Museum of Art.
 Returning from the Fields: oil on canvas 18¾″ × 26⅞″
 (47.6cm × 68.3cm). Signed and dated lower right: 1851. Be-
 quest of Mrs. W. F. Goodspeed.
 Sheep Grazing: oil on canvas 16¼″ × 20″ (41.3cm × 50.8cm).
 N.d. Signed lower left. Gift of Mrs. Horace L. Chapman.
 Untitled (two cows resting): graphite and watercolor on paper
 6⅞″ × 10″ (17.5cm × 25.4cm). Signed and dated lower left.
 Gift of Frederick W. Schumacher.

Oregon

Portland. Portland Art Museum.
  Black Sheep: watercolor 7⅜" × 10½".
  The Donkey: oil on canvas 18" × 14⅞".

Pennsylvania

Philadelphia. Philadelphia Museum of Art.
  Two Horses: oil on canvas 38½" × 51½". Signed lower right:
  Rosa Bonheur 1893. William L. Elkins Coll.
  Barbaro after the Hunt: oil on canvas 38" × 51¼". Signed
  lower right: Rosa Bonheur, inscribed upper right "Barbaro,"
  upper left "FL . . . [illegible]." W. P. Wilstach Coll.
  Pastoral—Landscape with Cattle: oil on canvas 33" × 48".
  Signed lower right: Rosa B. Given by Hermann and Edward
  Krumbhaar.

Reading. The Reading Public Museum and Art Gallery.
  Following the Plow: oil on canvas 26" × 36". Gift of Mrs.
  William L. Savage, 1921.

Rhode Island

Providence. Museum of Art, Rhode Island School of Design.
  Seven Horses: pencil on paper 9⁹⁄₁₆" × 13½" (25.5cm ×
  35.3cm). Bequest of Frederick Kinyon.

Virginia

Norfolk. Chrysler Museum at Norfolk.
  Cow: pencil drawing, sheet, 7¾" × 9⅞". Gift of Walter P.
  Chrysler. Red wax stamp on frame verso "Vente Rosa
  Bonheur 1900."

Wisconsin

Milwaukee. Milwaukee Art Center.
  Two Goats: oil on canvas 36¾" × 28⅝". Undated, but probably late.

Wyoming

Cody. Buffalo Bill Historical Center.
Col. William F. Cody: oil on canvas 18½″ × 15¼″. 1889.

In Foreign Collections:

Canada

Toronto. Art Gallery of Ontario.
Oxen: oil on canvas 14¼″ × 22″ (36.2cm × 55.9cm). Signed lower right corner. Bequest of John Paris Bickell 1952.

England

Liverpool. Walker Art Gallery.
Sheep and Lambs: panel 33cm × 43.5cm. Signed: Rosa Bonheur 1886.
Arab and Dead Horse: canvas 20cm × 34cm. Signed: R. Bonheur 1852.
Le Retour du Moulin: canvas 27.3cm × 35.5cm. Signed: Rosa Bonheur.
London. Wallace Collection.
A Waggon and Team of Horses: canvas 34.9cm × 62.5cm. Inscribed in lower right: Rosa Bonheur 1852.
Sheep: canvas 46.4cm × 65.1cm. Inscribed in lower left corner: Rosa Bonheur 57.
A Shepherd's Dog: canvas 46.4cm × 38.1cm. Inscribed in lower right corner: R. B. 64, in upper right corner "BRIZO."
Roe-Deer: panel 19.1cm × 24.8cm. Signed in lower left corner: Rosa Bonheur.
Sheffield. City Art Galleries.
Sheep in a Landscape: oil on canvas 10⅜″ × 14¼″. Signed: Rosa Bonheur.
A Stray Shot (with Landseer): oil on canvas 47½″ × 55½″. Signed and inscribed "Etude de Sir Edwin Landseer, paysage de Madmse. Rosa Bonheur."
Self Portrait: oil on panel, circular 5 in. diameter. Signed: Bonheur 1854.

France

Bordeaux. Musée et Galerie des Beaux-Arts.
Etude de renard: canvas
Tête de cheval: canvas
Les Lapins: canvas
Five drawings representing heads of dogs
Six bronzes:
   a ram
   two sheep
   three bulls
Tête de Bouc: canvas
Tête de chien: canvas
Fontainebleau. Musée National du Château de Fontainebleau.
Labourage Nivernais: 173cm × 260cm
La fenaison en Auvergne: 215cm × 422cm
La foulaison du blé en Camargue: 313cm × 654cm
Paysage: 26cm × 37cm
Paysage: 24cm × 35cm
Etude de forêt: 37cm × 27cm
Les boeufs roux: 37cm × 27cm
Etude de cheval bai cerise: 42cm × 34cm
Etude de cheval blanc: 30cm × 34cm
Etude de cheval gris: 82cm × 100cm (deposited at the Rosa
Bonheur studio at By-Thomery)
Chien de berger assis: 26cm × 18cm
Bélier: 21cm × 19cm
Deux tigres: 67cm × 73cm
Chêne: 28cm × 39cm
Etude de bélier: 28cm × 31cm
Etude de cerf: 44cm × 54cm
Etude cerf vu de dos: 18cm × 12cm
Etude de cheval bai: 12cm × 15cm
Etude de chèvre vue de dos: 18cm × 15cm
   Among these studies the only finished canvases are the first
two.
Grenoble. Musée Grenoble.
Boeuf en liberté: oil on canvas 55cm × 50cm. Signed lower
left: Rosa Bonheur.
Chantilly. Musée Condé.
Berger des Pyrénées

Langres. Musée du Breuil de Saint-Germain.
  Etude de lionne: 47cm × 53cm.
  Plateau près des cimes: 28cm × 41cm.
  Le coin du lac: 31cm × 41cm.
Lille. Musée des Beaux-Arts de Lille.
  Le Pâturage: oil on canvas 32cm × 48cm.
  Bergers landais: oil on canvas 24cm × 27cm.
Rouen. Musées de Rouen.
  Cheval blanc dans un pré: oil on canvas 34cm × 50cm. Signed lower left: Rosa B. Bought at the Rosa Bonheur sale 1900.

INDEX

ILLUSTRATIONS

Labourages Nivernais. John and Mable Ringling Museum of Art, Sarasota, Fla.

Sheep by the Sea. Norton Simon Museum of Art, Pasadena.

Col. William F. Cody. **Courtesy of the Buffalo Bill Historical Center, Cody, Wyo.**

King of the Forest. **The Warner Collection of the Gulf States Paper Corp., Tuscaloosa, Ala.**

The Duel. **The Warner Collection of the Gulf States Paper Corp., Tuscaloosa, Ala.**

Calves. Haussner's Restaurant, Baltimore, Md.

Two Horses. From the George P. Tweed Memorial Art Collection, The Tweed Museum of Art, University of Minnesota–Duluth, Duluth, Minn.

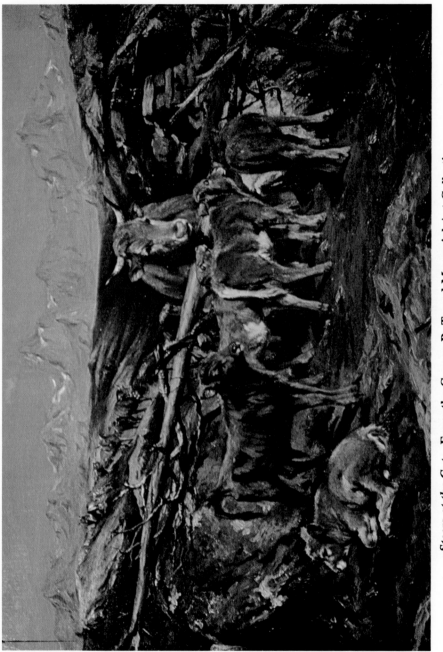

Steers at the Gate. From the George P. Tweed Memorial Art Collection, The Tweed Museum of Art, University of Minnesota–Duluth, Duluth, Minn.

Plowing Scene. The Walters Art Gallery, Baltimore.

65

Cattle at Rest on Hillside. **Courtesy of the Art Institute of Chicago.**

Does at Rest. The Currier Gallery of Art, Manchester, N.H.

Untitled (horse). Collection of the Phoenix Art Museum. Bequest of Dr. Patricia Lynch.

Relay Hunting. The Saint Louis Art Museum. Saint Louis, Mo.

Recumbent Stag. The Cleveland Museum of Art. Purchase, James Parmelee Fund.

Farmyard. The Cleveland Museum of Art. Gift of Mrs. John B. Dempsey.

71

Deer on the Alert. Courtesy of New Orleans Museum of Art, New Orleans, La.

Head of a Royal Tiger. Permission of the Fine Arts Museums of San Francisco.

Lioness's Heads. Permission of the Fine Arts Museums of San Francisco.

Studies of Two Male Figures. **Permission of the Fine Arts Museums of San Francisco.**

75

Stag on Watch. Permission of the Fine Arts Museums of San Francisco.

76

A Donkey Driver. **Permission of the Fine Arts Museums of San Francisco.**

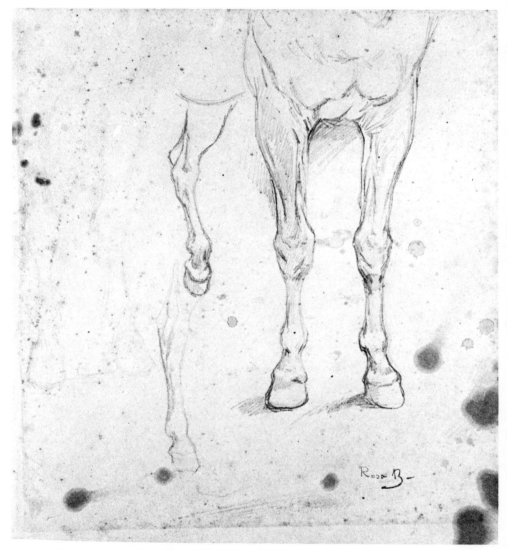

Horse's Legs. **San Diego Museum of Art. Gift of Mrs. Irving T. Snyder.**

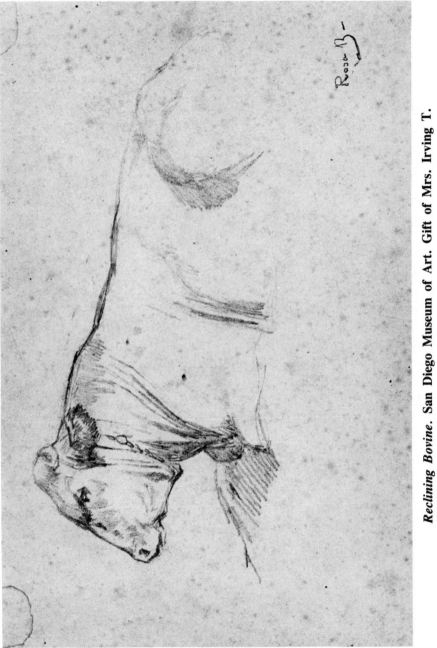

Reclining Bovine. San Diego Museum of Art. Gift of Mrs. Irving T. Snyder.

Bovine Head. San Diego Museum of Art. Gift of Mrs. Irving T. Snyder.

Asparagus. State University of New York at Buffalo.

Radishes. State University of New York at Buffalo.

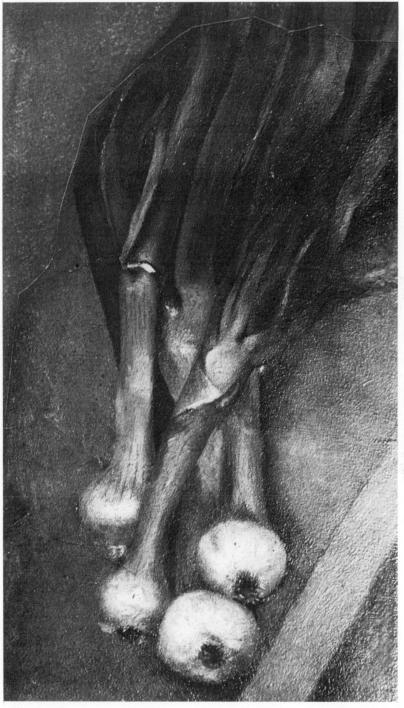

Green Onions. State University of New York at Buffalo.

Studies of Horsemen. The Art Museum, Princeton University. The Laura P. Hall Memorial Fund.

84

Study of a Dog. **The Art Museum, Princeton University. Gift of Stuart P. Feld.**

White Horse. The Art Museum, Princeton University. Gift of Edward Plaut.

Warrior Driving a Chariot. The Art Museum, Princeton University. The Laura P. Hall Memorial Fund.

87

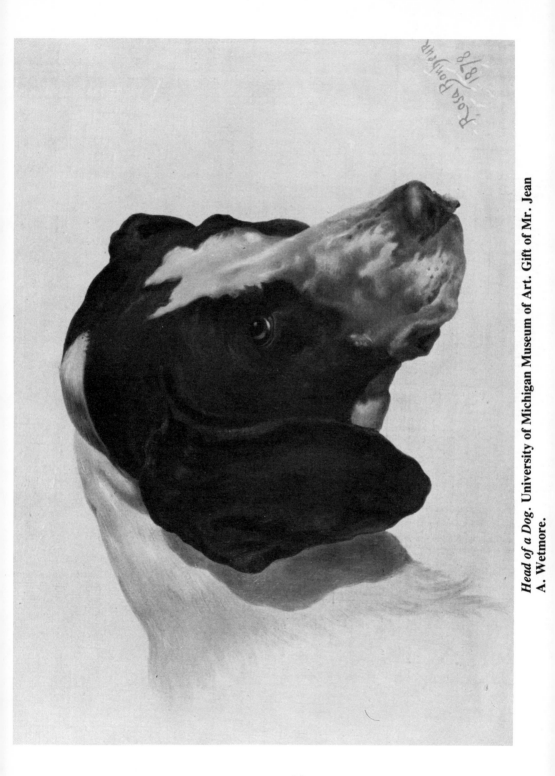

Head of a Dog. University of Michigan Museum of Art. Gift of Mr. Jean A. Wetmore.

Stag Listening to the Wind. Vassar College Art Gallery. Gift of Dexter Mason Ferry, Jr.

The Horse Fair. The Metropolitan Museum of Art. Gift of Cornelius Vanderbilt, 1887.

Study for *The Horse Fair*. The Metropolitan Museum of Art. Bequest of Edith H. Proskauer, 1975.

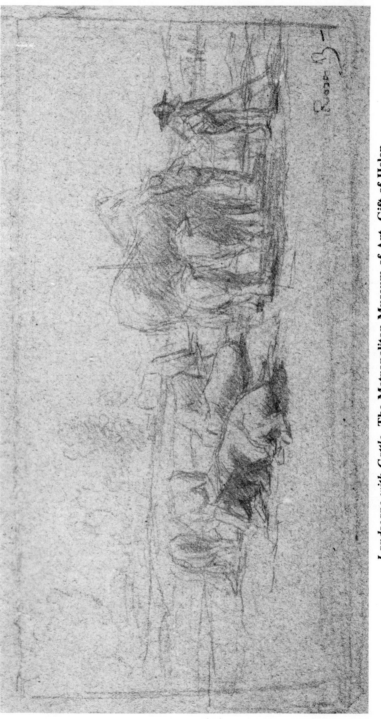

Landscape with Cattle. The Metropolitan Museum of Art. Gift of Helen Wormaer, 1963.

Young Bulls. Herbert F. Johnson Museum of Art, Cornell University.
Bequest of William P. Chapman.

Following the Plow. Courtesy of the Reading Public Museum and Art Gallery, Reading, Pa.

Cow. The Chrysler Museum, Norfolk, Va.

Head of a Bull. The Brooklyn Museum. Gift of John Hill Morgan.

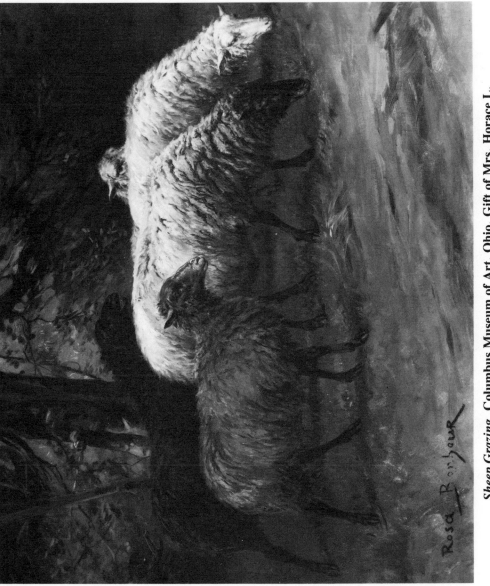

Sheep Grazing. Columbus Museum of Art, Ohio. Gift of Mrs. Horace L. Chapman.

Untitled (two cows resting). Columbus Museum of Art, Ohio. Gift of Frederick W. Schumacher.

Returning from the Fields. Columbus Museum of Art, Ohio. Bequest of Mrs. W. F. Goodspeed.

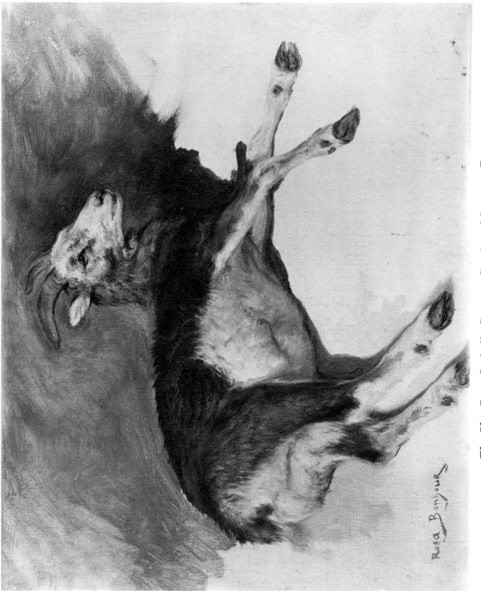

The She-Goat. Isabella Stewart Gardner Museum, Boston.

Study of a Lion's Head. Sterling and Francine Clark Art Institute, Williamstown, Mass.

Two Horses. The Philadelphia Museum of Art, William L. Elkins Collec-tion.

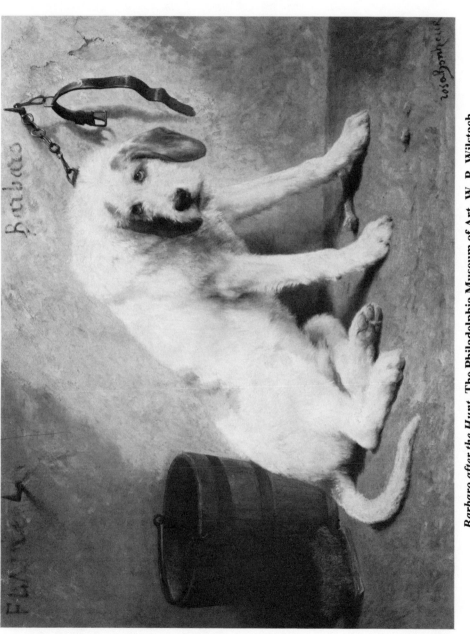

Barbaro after the Hunt. **The Philadelphia Museum of Art, W. P. Wilstach Collection.**

Pastoral Landscape with Cattle. The Philadelphia Museum of Art. Given by Edward Krumbhaar and Herman Krumbhaar.

Sheep. The Cleveland Museum of Art, Hinman B. Hurlbut Collection.

Boeufs et taureaux de la race du Cantal. Courtesy of the R. W. Norton Art Gallery, Shreveport, La.

La Fenaison en Auvergne. Courtesy of the R. W. Norton Art Gallery, Shreveport, La.

Muletiers des Pyrénées. Courtesy of the R. W. Norton Art Gallery, Shreveport, La.

Cow. Courtesy of the R. W. Norton Art Gallery, Shreveport, Louisiana.

Bull Reclining. **Courtesy of the R. W. Norton Art Gallery, Shreveport, Louisiana.**

Ewe Grazing. **Courtesy of the R. W. Norton Art Gallery, Shreveport, Louisiana.**